My Garden
of Prayer

Beloved Prayer Poetry from
HELEN STEINER RICE

Published by Barbour Books, an imprint of Barbour Publishing, Inc., P.O. Box 719, Uhrichsville, Ohio 44683, www.barbourbooks.com

Our mission is to publish and distribute inspirational products offering exceptional value and biblical encouragement to the masses.

 Member of the
Evangelical Christian
Publishers Association

Printed in China.

My Garden
of Prayer

Beloved Prayer Poetry from
HELEN STEINER RICE

BARBOUR BOOKS
An Imprint of Barbour Publishing, Inc.

Contents

Introduction

MY GARDEN OF PRAYER

My garden beautifies my yard and adds fragrance to the air,
But it is also my cathedral and my quiet place of prayer.
So little do we realize that the glory and the power
Of Him who made the universe lies hidden in a flower!

—HELEN STEINER RICE

Helen Steiner Rice's prayer life was living and active, as evidenced by the personal nature of her poetry. Many of her poems are prayers she penned directly to her heavenly Father, while others were prayers for special people in her life, and more still celebrated the privilege of and power that we have in prayer.

Here in this beautiful book, you'll find nearly one hundred of Helen's prayer poems. We believe that these simple, insightful words from her heart will strike a chord in your own faith and prayer life. A scripture from the King James Bible accompanies each prayer. We hope you enjoy these encouraging, thoughtful, challenging prayers and poems and that they draw you closer to the Lord in prayer.

Special Occasions

Let us therefore come boldly unto the throne of grace, that we may obtain mercy, and find grace to help in time of need.

HEBREWS 4:16

A NEW YEAR'S EVE PRAYER

What better time and what better season,
What greater occasion or more wonderful reason
To kneel down in prayer and lift our hands high
To the God of creation, who made earth and sky,
Who sent us His Son to live here among men—
And the message He brought is as true now as then. . .
So at this glad season, when there's joy everywhere,
Let us meet our Redeemer at the altar of prayer,
Asking Him humbly to bless all of our days
And grant us forgiveness for our erring ways. . .
And though we're unworthy, dear Father above,
Accept us today and let us dwell in Thy love,
So we may grow stronger upheld by Thy grace,
And with Thy assistance be ready to face
All the temptations that fill every day,
And hold on to our hands when we stumble and stray. . .
And thank You, dear God, for the year that now ends
And for the great blessing of loved ones and friends.

Remember ye not the former things,
neither consider the things of old.
Behold, I will do a new thing.

Isaiah 43:18–19

A NEW YEAR! A NEW DAY!
A NEW LIFE!

Not only on New Year's but all the year through
God gives us a chance to begin life anew,
For each day at dawning we have but to pray
That all the mistakes that we made yesterday
Will be blotted out and forgiven by grace,
For God in His love will completely efface
All that is past, and He'll grant a new start
To all who are truly repentant at heart.

Therefore if any man be in Christ,
he is a new creature: old things are passed away;
behold, all things are become new.

2 CORINTHIANS 5:17

A NEW YEAR BRINGS
A NEW BEGINNING

As the New Year starts and the old year ends
There's no better time to make amends
For all the things we sincerely regret
And wish in our hearts we could somehow forget—
We all make mistakes, for it's human to err,
But no one need ever give up in despair,
For God gives us all a brand-new beginning,
A chance to start over and repent of our sinning—
And when God forgives us we, too, must forgive
And resolve to do better each day that we live
By constantly trying to be like Him more nearly
And to trust in His wisdom and love Him more dearly—
Assured that we're never out of His care
And we're always welcome to seek Him in prayer.

Wherefore he saith, Awake thou
that sleepest, and arise from the dead,
and Christ shall give thee light.

EPHESIANS 5:14

LITTLE SPRINGTIME PRAYER

God, grant this little springtime prayer
And make our hearts, grown cold with care,
Once more aware of the waking earth
Now pregnant with life and bursting with birth.
For how can man feel any fear or doubt
When on every side all around and about
The March winds blow across man's face
And whisper of God's power and grace?
Oh, give us faith to believe again
That peace on earth, goodwill to men
Will follow this winter of man's mind
And awaken his heart and make him kind.
And just as great nature sends the spring
To give new birth to each sleeping thing,
God, grant rebirth to man's slumbering soul
And help him forsake his selfish goal.

*Her children arise up,
and call her blessed; her husband also,
and he praiseth her.*

Proverbs 31:28

A MOTHER'S DAY PRAYER

Our Father in heaven, whose love is divine,
Thanks for the love of a mother like mine.
In Thy great mercy look down from above
And grant this dear mother the gift of Your love,
And all through the year, whatever betide her,
Assure her each day that You are beside her.
And, Father in heaven, show me the way
To lighten her tasks and brighten her day,
And bless her dear heart with the insight to see
That her love means more than the world to me.

Children's children are the crown of old men;
and the glory of children are their fathers.

PROVERBS 17:6

MY FATHER'S DAY PRAYER

I said a Father's Day prayer for you—
I asked the Lord above
To keep you safely in His care
And enfold you in His love.
I did not ask for fortune,
For riches or for fame;
I only asked for blessings
In the Holy Savior's name—
Blessings to surround you
In times of trial and stress,
And inner joy to fill your heart
With peace and happiness.

The voice of joy, and the voice of gladness, the voice of the bridegroom, and the voice of the bride, the voice of them that shall say, Praise the LORD of hosts: for the LORD is good.

JEREMIAH 33:11

A PRAYER FOR THE BRIDE AND GROOM

As hand in hand you enter a life that's bright and new,
May God look down from heaven and bless the two of you.
May He give you understanding, enough to make you kind,
So you may judge each other with your
hearts and not your minds.
May He teach you to be patient as you learn to live together,
Forgiving little human rifts that arise in stormy weather.
And may your love be strong enough to
withstand the strongest sea,
So you may dwell forever in love's rich tranquility.

Enter into his gates with thanksgiving,
and into his courts with praise:
be thankful unto him, and bless his name.

PSALM 100:4

A THANKSGIVING DAY PRAYER

Faith of our fathers, renew us again
And make us a nation of God-fearing men
Seeking Thy guidance, Thy love, and Thy will,
For we are but pilgrims in search of Thee still. . .
And gathered together on Thanksgiving Day,
May we lift up our hearts and our hands as we pray
To thank You for blessings we so little merit,
And grant us Thy love and teach us to share it.

And the angel said unto them, Fear not: for, behold, I bring you good tidings of great joy, which shall be to all people. For unto you is born this day in the city of David a Saviour, which is Christ the Lord.

Luke 2:10–11

THE MIRACLE OF CHRISTMAS

The wonderment in a small child's eyes,
The ageless awe in the Christmas skies,
That nameless joy that fills the air,
The throngs that kneel in praise and prayer. . .
These are the things that make us know
That men may come and men may go,
But none will ever find a way
To banish Christ from Christmas Day. . .
For with each child there's born again
A mystery that baffles men.

For unto us a child is born, unto us a son is given: and the government shall be upon his shoulder: and his name shall be called Wonderful, Counsellor, The mighty God, The everlasting Father, The Prince of Peace.

ISAIAH 9:6

GOD IS ALWAYS THERE
TO HEAR OUR PRAYER

Let us find joy in the news of His birth,
And let us find comfort and strength for each day
In knowing that Christ walked this same earthly way,
So He knows all our needs and He hears every prayer,
And He keeps all His children always safe in His care. . .
And whenever we're troubled and lost in despair,
We have but to seek Him and ask Him in prayer
To guide and direct us and help us to bear
Our sickness and sorrow, our worry and care. . .
So once more at Christmas let the whole world rejoice
In the knowledge He answers every prayer that we voice.

Wherefore I also. . .cease not to give thanks for you, making mention of you in my prayers; that the God of our Lord Jesus Christ, the Father of glory, may give unto you the spirit of wisdom and revelation in the knowledge of him: the eyes of your understanding being enlightened; that ye may know what is the hope of his calling, and what the riches of the glory of his inheritance in the saints.

EPHESIANS 1:15–18

GIVE US DAILY AWARENESS

On life's busy thoroughfares
We meet with angels unaware
So Father, make us kind and wise
So we may always recognize
The blessings that are ours to take,
The friendships that are ours to make
If we but open our heart's door wide
To let the sunshine of love inside
For God is not in far distant places
But in loving hearts and friendly faces.

In the Morning. . .
Noon, and Night

And in the morning, rising up a great while before day, [Jesus] went out, and departed into a solitary place, and there prayed.

MARK 1:35

I MEET GOD IN THE MORNING

Each day at dawning I lift my heart high
And raise up my eyes to the infinite sky.
I watch the night vanish as a new day is born,
And I hear the birds sing on the wings of the morn.
I see the dew glisten in crystal-like splendor,
While God, with a touch that is gentle and tender,
Wraps up the night and softly tucks it away
And hangs out the sun to herald a new day. . .
And so I give thanks and my heart kneels to pray,
"God, keep me and guide me and go with me today."

My voice shalt thou hear in the morning,
O LORD; in the morning will I direct
my prayer unto thee, and will look up.

PSALM 5:3

BEGIN EACH DAY BY
KNEELING TO PRAY

Start every day with a "good morning" prayer
And God will bless each thing you do
and keep you in His care. . .
And never, never sever the spirit's silken strand
That our Father up in heaven holds
in His mighty hand.

Yet the LORD will command his
lovingkindness in the day time, and in
the night his song shall be with me,
and my prayer unto the God of my life.

PSALM 42:8

BREAKFAST FOR THE SOUL

I meet God in the morning and go with Him through the day,
Then in the stillness of the night before sleep comes I pray
That God will just take over all the problems I couldn't solve,
And in the peacefulness of sleep my cares will all dissolve.
So when I open up my eyes to greet another day,
I'll find myself renewed in strength and there will open up a way
To meet what seemed impossible for me to solve alone,
And once again I'll be assured I am never on my own.

It is a good thing to give thanks unto the LORD, and to sing praises unto thy name, O Most High: to shew forth thy lovingkindness in the morning, and thy faithfulness every night. . .for thou, LORD, hast made me glad through thy work: I will triumph in the works of thy hands.

PSALM 92:1–2, 4

THE FIRST THING EVERY MORNING AND THE LAST THING EVERY NIGHT

Were you too busy this morning to quietly stop and pray?
Did you hurry and drink your coffee then frantically rush away,
Consoling yourself by saying, "God will always be there
Waiting to hear my petitions, ready to answer each prayer?"
It's true that the great, generous Savior forgives
our transgressions each day
And patiently waits for lost sheep who constantly seem to stray,
But moments of prayer once omitted in the busy rush of the day
Can never again be recaptured, for they silently slip away.
Strength is gained in the morning to endure the trials of the day
When we visit with God in person in a quiet and unhurried way,
For only through prayer that's unhurried
can the needs of the day be met,
And only in prayers said at evening
can we sleep without fears or regret. . .
So seek the Lord in the morning and never forget Him at night,
For prayer is an unfailing blessing
that makes every burden seem light.

*I thank my God upon every remembrance
of you, always in every prayer of mine
for you all making request with joy.*

PHILIPPIANS 1:3–4

I THINK OF YOU,
AND I PRAY FOR YOU, TOO

Often during a busy day
I pause for a minute to silently pray.
I mention the names of those I love
And treasured friends I am fondest of—
For it doesn't matter where we pray
If we honestly mean the words we say,
For God is always listening to hear
The prayers that are made by a heart that's sincere.

Cause me to hear thy lovingkindness in the morning; for in thee do I trust: cause me to know the way wherein I should walk; for I lift up my soul unto thee.

PSALM 143:8

I COME TO MEET YOU

I come to meet You, God, and as I linger here
I seem to feel You very near.
A rustling leaf, a rolling slope
Speak to my heart of endless hope.
The sun just rising in the sky,
The waking birdlings as they fly,
The grass all wet with morning dew
Are telling me I just met You. . .
And gently thus the day is born
As night gives way to breaking morn,
And once again I've met You, God,
And worshipped on Your holy sod. . .
For who could see the dawn break through
Without a glimpse of heaven and You?
For who but God could make the day
And softly put the night away?

But the end of all things is at hand:
be ye therefore sober, and watch unto prayer.

1 PETER 4:7

GOD'S STAIRWAY

Step by step we climb each day
Closer to God with each prayer we pray,
For the cry of the heart offered in prayer
Becomes just another spiritual stair
In the heavenly staircase leading us to
A beautiful place where we live anew. . .
So never give up for it's worth the climb
To live forever in endless time
Where the soul of man is safe and free
To live in love through eternity!

Evening, and morning, and at noon, will I
pray, and cry aloud: and he shall hear my voice.

PSALM 55:17

ANYWHERE IS A PLACE OF PRAYER IF GOD IS THERE

I have prayed on my knees in the morning,
I have prayed as I walked along,
I have prayed in the silence and darkness,
and I've prayed to the tune of a song. . .
I have prayed in a velvet, hushed forest
where the quietness calmed my fears.
I have prayed through suffering and heartache
when my eyes were blinded with tears.
I have prayed in churches and chapels,
cathedrals and synagogues, too,
But often I had the feeling
that my prayers were not getting through. . .
And I realized then that our Father
is not really concerned when we pray
Or impressed by our manner of worship
or the eloquent words that we say.
He is only concerned with our feelings,
and He looks deep into our hearts
And hears the cry of our souls' deep need
that no words could ever impart.

My meditation of him shall be sweet:
I will be glad in the LORD.

PSALM 104:34

THE PEACE OF MEDITATION

So we may know God better
And feel His quiet power,
Let us daily keep in silence
A meditation hour—
For to understand God's greatness
And to use His gifts each day
The soul must learn to meet Him
In a meditative way.
For our Father tells His children
That if they would know His will
They must seek Him in the silence
When all is calm and still. . .
For nature's greatest forces
Are found in quiet things
Like softly falling snowflakes
Drifting down on angels' wings,
Or petals dropping soundlessly
From a lovely full-blown rose.
So God comes closest to us
When our souls are in repose.

He shall call upon me, and I will answer him: I will be with him in trouble; I will deliver him, and honour him.

PSALM 91:15

DAILY PRAYERS ARE
HEAVEN'S STAIRS

The stairway rises heaven-high, the steps are dark and steep.
In weariness we climb them as we stumble, fall, and weep.
And many times we falter along the path of prayer,
Wondering if You hear us and if You really care.
Oh, give us some assurance; restore our faith anew,
So we can keep on climbing the stairs of prayer to You.
For we are weak and wavering, uncertain and unsure,
And only meeting You in prayer can help us to endure
All life's trials and troubles, its sickness, pain, and sorrow,
And give us strength and courage to face and meet tomorrow.

O come, let us worship and bow down:
let us kneel before the LORD our maker.

PSALM 95:6

AT MY MOTHER'S KNEE

I have worshipped in churches and chapels.
I have prayed in the busy street.
I have sought my God and found Him
Where the waves of the ocean beat.
I have knelt in a silent forest
In the shade of an ancient tree,
But the dearest of all my altars
Was raised at my mother's knee.
God, make me the woman of her vision
And purge me of all selfishness
And help keep me true to her standards
And help me to live and her to bless.
And then keep me a pilgrim forever
To the shrine at my mother's knee.

Be careful for nothing; but in every thing by prayer and supplication with thanksgiving let your requests be made known unto God.

PHILIPPIANS 4:6

DAILY PRAYERS
DISSOLVE YOUR CARES

We all have cares and problems we cannot solve alone,
But if we go to God in prayer, we are never on our own.
And if we try to stand alone, we are weak and we will fall,
For God is always greatest when we're helpless, lost, and small...
And no day is unmeetable if on rising, our first thought
Is to thank God for the blessings that His loving care has brought.
For there can be no failures or hopeless, unsaved sinners
If we enlist the help of God, who makes all losers winners...
So meet Him in the morning and go with Him through the day
And thank Him for His guidance each evening when you pray—
And if you follow faithfully this daily way to pray,
You will never in your lifetime face another hopeless day...
For like a soaring eagle, you, too, can rise above
The storms of life around you on the wings of prayer and love.

*Even them will I bring to my holy mountain,
and make them joyful in my house of prayer.*

Isaiah 56:7

THE HEAVENLY STAIRCASE

Prayers are the stairs that lead to God,
and there's joy every step of the way
When we make our pilgrimage to Him
with love in our hearts each day.

Take my yoke upon you, and learn of me;
for I am meek and lowly in heart:
and ye shall find rest unto your souls.

MATTHEW 11:29

LEARN TO REST

We all need short vacations in life's fast and maddening race
An interlude of quietness from the constant, jet-age pace.
So when your day is pressure-packed
and your hours are all too few,
Just close your eyes and meditate and let God talk to you.
For when we keep on pushing, we're not following in God's way;
We are foolish, selfish robots mechanized to fill each day
With unimportant trivia that makes life more complex
And gives us greater problems to irritate and vex.
So when your nervous network becomes a tangled mess,
Just close your eyes in silent prayer and ask the Lord to bless
Each thought that you are thinking, each decision you must make,
As well as every word you speak and every step you take.
For only by the grace of God can you gain self-control,
And only meditative thoughts can restore your peace and soul.

I cry unto thee daily. Rejoice the soul of thy servant: for unto thee, O Lord, do I lift up my soul.

PSALM 86:3–4

INSPIRATION! MEDITATION! DEDICATION!

Brighten your day
And lighten your way
And lessen your cares
With daily prayers.
Quiet your mind
And leave tension behind
And find inspiration
In hushed meditation.

Prayer's Divine Purpose

For it is God which worketh in you both
to will and to do of his good pleasure.

PHILIPPIANS 2:13

NOT WHAT YOU WANT
BUT WHAT GOD WANTS

Do you want what you want when you want it?
Do you pray and expect a reply?
And when it's not instantly answered
Do you feel that God passed you by?
Well, prayers that are prayed in this manner
Are really not prayers at all,
For you can't go to God in a hurry
And expect Him to answer your call.
For prayers are not meant for obtaining
What we selfishly wish to acquire,
For God in His wisdom refuses
The things that we wrongly desire. . .
Wake up! You are missing completely
The reason and purpose of prayer,
Which is really to keep us contented
That God holds us safe in His care.
And God only answers our pleadings
When He knows that our wants fill a need,
And whenever our will becomes His will,
There is no prayer that God does not heed!

When thou prayest, enter into thy closet,
and when thou hast shut thy door, pray to thy
Father which is in secret; and thy Father
which seeth in secret shall reward thee openly.

MATTHEW 6:6

WHAT IS PRAYER?

Is it measured words that are memorized,
Forcefully said and dramatized,
Offered with pomp and with arrogant pride
In words unmatched to the feelings inside?
No, prayer is so often just words unspoken,
Whispered in tears by a heart that is broken,
For God is already deeply aware
Of the burdens we find too heavy to bear. . .
And all we need do is seek Him in prayer
And without a word He will help us to bear
Our trials and troubles, our sickness and sorrow
And show us the way to a brighter tomorrow.
There's no need at all for impressive prayer,
For the minute we seek God, He's already there.

*It is written, My house shall
be called the house of prayer.*

MATTHEW 21:13

THE HOUSE OF PRAYER

Just close your eyes and open your heart
And feel your cares and worries depart.
Just yield yourself to the Father above
And let Him hold you secure in His love. . .
For life on earth grows more involved
With endless problems that can't be solved,
But God only asks us to do our best—
Then He will take over and finish the rest. . .
So when you are tired, discouraged, and blue,
There's always one door that is opened to you
And that is the door to the house of prayer,
And you'll find God waiting to meet you there. . .
And the house of prayer is no farther away
Than the quiet spot where you kneel and pray.
For the heart is a temple when God is there
As we place ourselves in His loving care. . .
And He hears every prayer and answers each one
When we pray in His name, "Thy will be done."
And the burdens that seemed too heavy to bear
Are lifted away on the wings of prayer.

The righteous cry, and the *LORD* heareth,
and delivereth them out of all their troubles.

PSALM 34:17

NO PRAYER GOES UNHEARD

Often we pause and wonder when we kneel down and pray,
Can God really hear the prayers that we say?
But if we keep praying and talking to Him,
He'll brighten the soul that was clouded and dim.
And as we continue, our burden seems lighter,
Our sorrow is softened, and our outlook is brighter.
For though we feel helpless and alone when we start,
A prayer is the key that opens the heart,
And as the heart opens, the dear Lord comes in.
And the prayer that we felt we could never begin
Is so easy to say, for the Lord understands
And He gives us new strength by the touch of His hands.

For which cause we faint not; but though
our outward man perish, yet the inward
man is renewed day by day.

2 CORINTHIANS 4:16

RENEWAL

When life has lost its luster and it's filled with dull routine,
When you long to run away from it,
seeking pastures new and green,
Remember, no one runs away from life
without finding when they do
That you can't escape the thoughts you think
that are pressing down on you.
For though the scenery may be different,
it's the same old heart and mind
And the same old restless longings
that you tried to leave behind. . .
So when your heart is heavy and your day is dull with care,
Instead of trying to escape, why not withdraw in prayer?
For in prayer there is renewal of the spirit, mind, and heart,
For everything is lifted up in which God has a part.
For when we go to God in prayer, our thoughts are rearranged,
So even though our problems have not been solved or changed,
Somehow the good Lord gives us the power to understand
That He who holds tomorrow is the One who holds our hands.

For God is my witness, whom I serve
with my spirit in the gospel of his Son,
that without ceasing I make mention
of you always in my prayers.

ROMANS 1:9

HEART SONG

There are so many, many times God seems so far away
That I can't help but wonder if He hears me when I pray.
Then I beseech Him earnestly to hear my humble plea
And tell me how to serve Him and to do it gallantly. . .
And so I pray this little prayer and hope that He will show me
How I can bring more happiness to all the folks who know me,
And give me hope and courage, enough for every day,
And faith to light the darkness when I stumble on my way,
And love and understanding, enough to make me kind,
So I may judge all people with my heart and not my mind.

Your Father knoweth what things
ye have need of, before ye ask him.

Matthew 6:8

GOD ALREADY KNOWS

Beyond that which words can interpret or theology can explain
The world feels a shower of refreshment
that falls like the gentle rain
On hearts that are parched with problems
and are searching to find the way
To somehow attract God's attention
through well-chosen words as they pray—
Not knowing that God in His wisdom
can sense all man's worry and woe,
For there is nothing man can conceal
that God does not already know. . .
So kneel in prayer in His presence
and you'll find no need to speak,
For softly in silent communion
God grants you the peace that you seek.

Rest in the LORD, and wait patiently for him.

PSALM 37:7

HE UNDERSTANDS

Although it sometimes seems to us
our prayers have not been heard,
God always knows our every need without a single word.
And He will not forsake us even though the way is steep,
For always He is near to us, a tender watch to keep. . .
And in good time He will answer us,
and in His love He'll send
Greater things than we have asked
and blessings without end. . .
So though we do not understand why trouble comes to man,
Can we not be contented just to know it is God's plan?

But we will give ourselves continually to prayer, and to the ministry of the word.

THE POWER OF PRAYER

I am only a worker employed by the Lord,
And great is my gladness and rich my reward
If I can just spread the wonderful story
That God is the answer to eternal glory. . .
And only the people who read my poems
Can help me to reach more hearts and homes,
Bringing new hope and comfort and cheer,
Telling sad hearts there is nothing to fear,
And what greater joy could there be than to share
The love of God and the power of prayer.

*If it be possible, as much as lieth in you,
live peaceably with all men.*

ROMANS 12:18

THE HEART OF "ME"

Teach us to walk humbly and closer in Thy ways,
And give us faith and courage to put purpose in our days.
And make each one of us aware that each must do his part,
For in the individual is where peace must have its start.
For a better world to live in where all are safe and free
Must start with faith and hope and love
deep in the heart of "me."

There is neither Jew nor Greek, there is neither
bond nor free, there is neither male nor female:
for ye are all one in Christ Jesus.

GALATIANS 3:28

COMMON GROUND

Father, make us kind and wise
So we may come to realize
That God the Father made us all—
The rich, the poor, the great, the small—
And in the Father's holy sight,
No one is yellow, black, or white.
And peace on earth cannot be found
Until we meet on common ground.
Great is our gladness to serve God through others,
For our Father taught us we are all sisters and brothers.

But this I say, He which soweth sparingly shall reap also sparingly; and he which soweth bountifully shall reap also bountifully.

2 CORINTHIANS 9:6

PRAYERS CAN'T BE ANSWERED
UNTIL THEY ARE PRAYED

Life without purpose is barren indeed;
There can't be a harvest unless you plant seed.
There can't be attainment unless there's a goal,
And man's but a robot unless there's a soul.
If we send no ships out, no ships will come in,
And unless there's a contest, nobody can win. . .
For games can't be won unless they are played,
And prayers can't be answered unless they are prayed. . .
So whatever is wrong with your life today,
You'll find a solution if you kneel down and pray
Not just for pleasure, enjoyment, and health,
Not just for honors, prestige, and wealth,
But pray for a purpose to make life worth living,
And pray for the joy of unselfish giving. . .
For great is your gladness and rich your reward
When you make your life's purpose the choice of the Lord.

But now, O LORD, thou art our father;
we are the clay, and thou our potter;
and we all are the work of thy hand.

Isaiah 64:8

MORE OF THEE, LESS OF ME

Take me and break me and make me, dear God,
just what You want me to be.
Give me the strength to accept what You send
and eyes with the vision to see
All the small, arrogant ways that I have
and the vain little things that I do.
Make me aware that I'm often concerned
more with myself than with You.
Uncover before me my weakness and greed
and help me to search deep inside
So I may discover how easy it is
to be selfishly lost in my pride.
And then in Thy goodness and mercy,
look down on this weak, erring one
And tell me that I am forgiven for all I've so willfully done,
And teach me to humbly start following
the path that the dear Savior trod
So I'll find at the end of life's journey
a home in the city of God.

Open thou mine eyes, that I may behold
wondrous things out of thy law.

PSALM 119:18

WIDEN MY VISION

God, open my eyes so I may see
And feel Your presence close to me.
Give me strength for my stumbling feet
As I battle the crowd on life's busy street,
And widen the vision of my unseeing eyes
So in passing faces I'll recognize
Not just a stranger, unloved and unknown,
But a friend with a heart that is much like my own.
Give me perception to make me aware
That scattered profusely on life's thoroughfare
Are the best gifts of God that we daily pass by
As we look at the world with an unseeing eye.

Shew me thy ways, O LORD;
teach me thy paths.

Psalm 25:4

MY PRAYER

Bless me, heavenly Father—forgive my erring ways.
Grant me strength to serve Thee; put purpose in my days.
Give me understanding, enough to make me kind,
So I may judge all people with my heart and not my mind.
Teach me to be patient in everything I do,
Content to trust Your wisdom and to follow after You.
Help me when I falter, and hear me when I pray,
And receive me in Thy kingdom to dwell with Thee someday.

Times of Uncertainty

The LORD is my shepherd; I shall not want. He maketh me to lie down in green pastures: he leadeth me beside the still waters.

PSALM 23:1–2

THE BLESSINGS OF
PATIENCE AND COMFORT

Realizing my helplessness,
I'm asking God if He will bless
The thoughts you think and all you do
So these dark hours you're passing through
Will lose their grave anxiety
And only deep tranquility
Will fill your mind and help impart
New strength and courage to your heart.
So take the Savior's loving hand
And do not try to understand—
Just let Him lead you where He will,
Through pastures green and waters still.
And though the way ahead seems steep,
Be not afraid for He will keep
Tender watch through night and day,
And He will hear each prayer you pray.

Be strong and of a good courage; be not afraid,
neither be thou dismayed: for the *LORD* thy
God is with thee whithersoever thou goest.

JOSHUA 1:9

NEVER BE DISCOURAGED

There is really nothing we need know or even try to understand
If we refuse to be discouraged and trust God's guiding hand.
So take heart and meet each minute with faith in God's great love,
Aware that every day of life is controlled by God above.
And never dread tomorrow or what the future brings,
Just pray for strength and courage and trust God in all things.
And never grow discouraged—be patient and just wait,
For God never comes too early, and He never comes too late.

And the LORD, he it is that doth go before thee; he will be with thee, he will not fail thee, neither forsake thee: fear not, neither be dismayed.

DEUTERONOMY 31:8

GOD WILL NOT FAIL YOU

When life seems empty and there's no place to go,
When your heart is troubled and your spirits are low,
When friends seem few and nobody cares,
There is always God to hear your prayers. . .
And whatever you're facing will seem much less
When you go to God and confide and confess.
For the burden that seems too heavy to bear
God lifts away on the wings of prayer. . .
And seen through God's eyes earthly troubles diminish,
And we're given new strength to face and to finish
Life's daily tasks as they come along
If we pray for strength to keep us strong. . .
So go to our Father when troubles assail you,
For His grace is sufficient, and He'll never fail you.

Ask, and it shall be given you; seek, and ye shall find; knock, and it shall be opened unto you.

Matthew 7:7

GOD IS NEVER
BEYOND OUR REACH

No one ever sought the Father and found He was not there,
And no burden is too heavy to be lightened by a prayer.
No problem is too intricate, and no sorrow that we face
Is too deep and devastating to be softened by His grace.
No trials and tribulations are beyond what we can bear
If we share them with our Father as we talk to Him in prayer. . .
And men of every color, every race, and every creed
Have but to seek the Father in their deepest hour of need.
God asks for no credentials—He accepts us with our flaws.
He is kind and understanding, and He welcomes us because
We are His erring children and He loves us, every one,
And He freely and completely forgives all that we have done,
Asking only if we're ready to follow where He leads,
Content that in His wisdom He will answer all our needs.

But ye, beloved, building up yourselves
on your most holy faith, praying in the
Holy Ghost, keep yourselves in the love
of God, looking for the mercy of our
Lord Jesus Christ unto eternal life.

JUDE 1:20–21

WINGS OF PRAYER

On the wings of prayer our burdens take flight
And our load of care becomes bearably light,
And our heavy hearts are lifted above
To be healed by the balm of God's wondrous love,
And the tears in our eyes are dried by the hands
Of a loving Father who understands
All of our problems, our fears and despair,
When we take them to Him on the wings of prayer.

They cry unto the LORD in their trouble,
and he bringeth them out of their distresses. He
maketh the storm a calm, so that the waves thereof
are still. Then are they glad because they be quiet;
so he bringeth them unto their desired haven.

PSALM 107:28–30

THOUGHTS OF PEACE

Whenever I am troubled and lost in deep despair
I bundle all my troubles up and go to God in prayer. . .
I tell Him I am heartsick, and lost and lonely, too,
That my heart is deeply burdened and
I don't know what to do. . .
But I know He stilled the tempest and calmed the angry sea,
And I humbly ask if in His love He'll do the same for me. . .
And then I just keep quiet and think only thoughts of peace,
And if I abide in stillness my restless murmurings cease.

Humble yourselves therefore under the
mighty hand of God, that he may exalt you
in due time: casting all your care upon him;
for he careth for you.

1 Peter 5:6–7

TALK IT OVER WITH GOD

You're worried and troubled about everything,
Wondering and fearing what tomorrow will bring.
You long to tell someone, for you feel so alone,
But your friends are all burdened with cares of their own.
There is only one place and only one friend
Who is never too busy, and you can always depend
On Him to be waiting with arms open wide
To hear all the troubles you came to confide. . .
For the heavenly Father will always be there
When you seek Him and find Him at the altar of prayer.

And he went a little farther, and fell on his face, and prayed, saying, O my Father, if it be possible, let this cup pass from me: nevertheless not as I will, but as thou wilt.

MATTHEW 26:39

THY WILL BE DONE

God did not promise sun without rain,
Light without darkness, or joy without pain.
He only promised strength for the day
When the darkness comes and we lose our way. . .
For only through sorrow do we grow more aware
That God is our refuge in times of despair.
For when we are happy and life's bright and fair,
We often forget to kneel down in prayer. . .
But God seems much closer and needed much more
When trouble and sorrow stand outside our door,
For then we seek shelter in His wondrous love,
And we ask Him to send us help from above. . .
And that is the reason we know it is true
That bright, shining hours and dark, sad ones, too,
Are part of the plan God made for each one,
And all we can pray is "Thy will be done."
And know that you are never alone,
For God is your Father and you're one of His own.

Let us lay aside every weight, and the sin which doth so easily beset us, and let us run with patience the race that is set before us, looking unto Jesus the author and finisher of our faith.

HEBREWS 12:1–2

A PRAYER FOR PEACE
AND PATIENCE

God, teach me to be patient, teach me to go slow.
Teach me how to wait on You when my way I do not know.
Teach me sweet forbearance, when things do not go right,
So I remain unruffled when others grow uptight.
Teach me how to quiet my racing, rising heart,
So I might hear the answer You are trying to impart.
Teach me to let go, dear God, and pray undisturbed until
My heart is filled with inner peace and I learn to know Your will.

Better is an handful with quietness, than both the hands full with travail and vexation of spirit.

ECCLESIASTES 4:6

LISTEN IN THE QUIETNESS

To try to run away from life is impossible to do,
For no matter where you chance to go,
your troubles will follow you;
For though the scenery is different,
when you look deep inside you'll find
The same deep, restless longings that
you thought you left behind.
So when life becomes a problem
much too great for us to bear,
Instead of trying to escape,
let us withdraw in prayer.
For withdrawal means renewal
if we withdraw to pray
And listen in the quietness
to hear what God will say.

I waited patiently for the LORD;
and he inclined unto me, and heard my cry.

PSALM 40:1

ANXIOUS PRAYERS

When we are deeply disturbed by a problem
and our minds are filled with doubt,
And we struggle to find a solution,
but there seems to be no way out,
We futilely keep on trying to untangle our web of distress,
But our own little, puny efforts meet with very little success.
And finally, exhausted and weary,
discouraged and downcast and low,
With no foreseeable answer and with no other place to go,
We kneel down in sheer desperation
and slowly and stumblingly pray,
Then impatiently wait for an answer in
one sudden instant, we say,
"God does not seem to be listening,
so why should we bother to pray?"
But God can't get through to the anxious,
who are much too impatient to wait.
You have to believe in God's promise
that He comes not too soon or too late,
For whether God answers promptly
or delays in answering your prayer,
You must have faith to believe Him
and to know in your heart He'll be there.

*Blessed are they that have not seen,
and yet have believed.*

John 20:29

FAITH AND TRUST

Sometimes when a light
Goes out of our lives
And we are left in darkness
And we do not know which way to go,
We must put our hand
Into the hand of God
And ask Him to lead us.
And if we let our lives become a prayer
Until we are strong enough
To stand under the weight
Of our own thoughts again,
Somehow, even the most difficult
Hours are bearable.

These things I have spoken unto you, that in me ye might have peace. In the world ye shall have tribulation: but be of good cheer; I have overcome the world.

JOHN 16:33

GOD IS THE ANSWER

We read the headlines daily, and we listen to the news;
We are anxious and bewildered
with the world's conflicting views.
We are restless and dissatisfied and sadly insecure,
And we voice our discontentment over things we must endure.
So instead of reading headlines that disturb the heart and mind,
Let us open up the Bible, for in doing so we'll find
That this age is no different from the millions gone before,
And in every hour of crisis God has opened up a door.
And though there's hate and violence and dissension all around,
We can always find a refuge that is built on solid ground.
So as we pray for guidance, may a troubled world revive
Faith in God and confidence so our nation may survive
And draw us ever closer to God and to each other
Until every stranger is a friend and every man a brother.

*My brethren, count it all joy when
ye fall into divers temptations.*

JAMES 1:2

THE WAY TO GOD

If my days were untroubled and my heart always light
Would I seek that fair land where there is no night?
If I never grew weary with the weight of my load
Would I search for God's peace at the end of the road?
If I never knew sickness and never felt pain
Would I reach for a hand to help and sustain?
If I walked not with sorrow and lived without loss
Would my soul seek sweet solace at the foot of the cross?
If all I desired was mine day by day
Would I kneel before God and earnestly pray?
If God sent no winter to freeze me with fear
Would I yearn for the warmth of spring every year?
I ask myself this and the answer is plain—
If my life were all pleasure and I never knew pain
I'd seek God less often and need Him much less.
For God's sought more often in times of distress,
And no one knows God or sees Him as plain
As those who have met Him on the pathway of pain.

Trust in the LORD with all thine heart;
and lean not unto thine own understanding.
In all thy ways acknowledge him,
and he shall direct thy paths.

PROVERBS 3:5–6

TRUST GOD

Take heart and meet each minute
with faith in God's great love,
Aware that every day of life
is controlled by God above. . .
And never dread tomorrow
or what the future brings—
Just pray for strength and courage
and trust God in all things.

Heavenly Blessings

Delight thyself also in the LORD: and he shall give thee the desires of thine heart.

PSALM 37:4

A SURE WAY TO A HAPPY DAY

Happiness is something we create in our minds—
It's not something you search for and so seldom find.
It's just waking up and beginning the day
By counting our blessings and kneeling to pray.
It's giving up thoughts that breed discontent
And accepting what comes as a gift heaven-sent.
It's giving up wishing for things we have not
And making the best of whatever we've got.
It's knowing that life is determined for us
And pursuing our tasks without fret, fume, or fuss. . .
For it's by completing what God gives us to do
That we find real contentment and happiness, too.

There shall be showers of blessing.

EZEKIEL 34:26

TAKE TIME TO APPRECIATE
GOD'S BLESSINGS

Blessings are all around us.
If we look we can recognize a blessing in
each day, each hour, each minute,
each family member, each friend, each neighbor,
each community, each city, each nation,
each challenge, each word of encouragement,
each flower, each sunbeam, each raindrop,
each awesome wonder crafted by God,
each star, each sea, each bird, each tree,
each sorrow, each disappointment,
each faith, each prayer.

Now the LORD had said unto Abram. . .
I will bless thee, and make thy name great;
and thou shalt be a blessing.

GENESIS 12:1–2

MAKE ME A CHANNEL
OF BLESSING TODAY

"Make me a channel of blessing today,"
I ask again and again when I pray.
Do I turn a deaf ear to the Master's voice
Or refuse to hear His direction and choice?
I only know at the end of the day
That I did so little to pay my way.

Now therefore let it please thee to bless the house of thy servant, that it may be before thee for ever: for thou blessest, O LORD, and it shall be blessed for ever.

1 CHRONICLES 17:27

BLESS THIS HOUSE

Dear God, let Thy peace be over all;
Let it hang from every wall.
Bless this house with joy and love;
Watch it from Your home above.
Bless this house and may it be
Forever in the care of Thee.

Let us draw near with a true heart in full assurance of faith. . . . for he is faithful that promised.

HEBREWS 10:22–23

GOD'S ASSURANCE GIVES US ENDURANCE

My blessings are so many, my troubles are so few—
How can I be discouraged when I know that I have You?
And I have the sweet assurance that there's nothing I need fear
If I but keep remembering I am Yours and You are near.
Help me to endure the storms that keep raging deep inside me,
And make me more aware each day that no evil can betide me.
If I remain undaunted though the billows sweep and roll,
Knowing I have Your assurance, there's a haven for my soul.
For anything and everything can somehow be endured
If Your presence is beside me and lovingly assured.

I beseech you therefore, brethren, by the mercies of God, that ye present your bodies a living sacrifice, holy, acceptable unto God, which is your reasonable service.

ROMANS 12:1

THIS IS ALL I ASK

Lord, show me the way
I can somehow repay
The blessings You've given to me. . .
Lord, teach me to do
What You most want me to
And to be what You want me to be. . .
I'm unworthy I know
But I do love You so—
I beg You to answer my plea. . .
I've not got much to give
But as long as I live
May I give it completely to Thee!

Which of you by taking thought can add one cubit unto his stature?

MATTHEW 6:27

MAKE YOUR DAY BRIGHT
BY THINKING RIGHT

Don't start your day by supposin' that trouble is just ahead.
It's better to stop supposin' and start with a prayer instead.
And make it a prayer of thanksgiving
for the wonderful things God has wrought,
Like the beautiful sunrise and sunset—
God's gifts that are free and not bought.
For what is the use of supposin'
that dire things could happen to you,
Worrying about some misfortune
that seldom if ever comes true.
But instead of just idle supposin',
step forward to meet each new day
Secure in the knowledge God's near you
to lead you each step of the way.
For supposin' the worst things will happen
only helps to make them come true,
And you darken the bright, happy moments
that the dear Lord has given to you.
So if you desire to be happy and get rid of the misery of dread,
Just give up supposin' the worst things
and look for the best things instead.

Unto thee, O God, do we give thanks,
unto thee do we give thanks: for that thy
name is near thy wondrous works declare.

PSALM 75:1

THINGS TO BE THANKFUL FOR

The good, green earth beneath our feet,
The air we breathe, the food we eat,
Some work to do, a goal to win,
A hidden longing deep within
That spurs us on to bigger things
And helps us meet what each day brings—
All these things and many more
Are things we should be thankful for. . .
And most of all, our thankful prayers
Should rise to God because He cares.

Be glad in the LORD, and rejoice,
ye righteous: and shout for joy,
all ye that are upright in heart.

PSALM 32:11

BE GLAD

Be glad that your life has been full and complete.
Be glad that you've tasted the bitter and sweet.
Be glad that you've walked in sunshine and rain.
Be glad that you've felt both pleasure and pain.
Be glad that you've had such a full, happy life.
Be glad for your joy as well as your strife.
Be glad that you've walked with courage each day.
Be glad you've had strength for each step of the way.
Be glad for the comfort that you've found in prayer.
Be glad for God's blessings, His love, and His care.

I am the good shepherd, and know my sheep,
and am known of mine.

John 10:14

MY GOD IS NO STRANGER

I've never seen God, but I know how I feel—
It's people like you who make Him so real.
My God is no stranger—He's so friendly each day,
And He doesn't ask me to weep when I pray.
It seems that I pass Him so often each day
In the faces of people I meet on my way.
He's the stars in the heavens, a smile on some face,
A leaf on a tree, or a rose in a vase.
He's winter and autumn and summer and spring—
In short, God is every real, wonderful thing.
I wish I might meet Him much more than I do—
I wish that there were more people like you.

In every thing give thanks: for this is the will of God in Christ Jesus concerning you.

1 Thessalonians 5:18

SO MANY REASONS
TO LOVE THE LORD

Thank You, God, for little things that come unexpectedly
To brighten up a dreary day that dawned so dismally.
Thank You, God, for sending a happy thought my way
To blot out my depression on a disappointing day.
Thank You, God, for brushing the dark clouds from my mind
And leaving only sunshine and joy of heart behind.
Oh God, the list is endless of the things to thank You for,
But I take them all for granted and unconsciously ignore
That everything I think or do, each movement that I make,
Each measured, rhythmic heartbeat, each breath of life I take
Is something You have given me for which there is no way
For me in all my smallness to in any way repay.

*Blessed be the Lord, who daily loadeth us
with benefits, even the God of our salvation.*

PSALM 68:19

A PRAYER OF THANKS

Thank You, God, for the beauty
around me everywhere,
The gentle rain and glistening dew,
the sunshine and the air,
The joyous gift of feeling
the soul's soft, whispering voice
That speaks to me from deep within
and makes my heart rejoice.

In thy presence is fulness of joy; at thy
right hand there are pleasures for evermore.

PSALM 16:11

NO FAVOR DO I SEEK TODAY

I come not to ask, to plead or implore You—
I just come to tell You how much I adore You.
For to kneel in Your presence makes me feel blessed,
For I know that You know all my needs best.
And it fills me with joy just to linger with You
As my soul You replenish and my heart You renew.
For prayer is much more than just asking for things—
It's the peace and contentment that quietness brings.
So thank You again for Your mercy and love
And for making me heir to Your kingdom above.

We are troubled on every side, yet not distressed;
we are perplexed, but not in despair. . . .
Knowing that he which raised up the
Lord Jesus shall raise up us also by
Jesus, and shall present us with you.

2 Corinthians 4:8, 14

NO ROOM FOR BLESSINGS

Refuse to be discouraged; refuse to be distressed.
For when we are despondent, our lives cannot be blessed.
Doubt and fear and worry close the door to faith and prayer,
And there's no room for blessings
when we're lost in deep despair.
So remember when you're troubled
with uncertainty and doubt,
It is best to tell our Father what our fear is all about.
For unless we seek His guidance when troubled times arise,
We are bound to make decisions that are twisted and unwise.
But when we view our problems
through the eyes of God above,
Misfortunes turn to blessings and hatred turns to love.

Being enriched in every thing to all bountifulness, which causeth through us thanksgiving to God.

2 CORINTHIANS 9:11

THANK YOU, GOD, FOR EVERYTHING

Thank You, God, for everything—
the big things and the small—
For every good gift comes from God, the giver of them all,
And all too often we accept without any thanks or praise
The gifts God sends as blessings each day in many ways.
And so at this time we offer up a prayer
To thank You, God, for giving us a lot more than our share.
First, thank You for the little things that often come our way—
The things we take for granted
and don't mention when we pray—
The unexpected courtesy, the thoughtful, kindly deed,
A hand reached out to help us in the time of sudden need.
Oh, make us more aware, dear God, of little daily graces
That come to us with sweet surprise
from never-dreamed-of places.
Then thank You for the miracles we are much too blind to see,
and give us new awareness of our many gifts from Thee.
And help us to remember that the key to life and living
Is to make each prayer a prayer of thanks and
each day a day of thanksgiving.

The Shadow of Thy Wings

Are not five sparrows sold for two farthings,
and not one of them is forgotten before God?
But even the very hairs of your head are all
numbered. Fear not therefore: ye are of
more value than many sparrows.

LUKE 12:6–7

SOMEBODY LOVES YOU

Somebody loves you more than you know.
Somebody goes with you wherever you go.
Somebody really and truly cares
And lovingly listens to all of your prayers. . .
Don't doubt for a minute that this is not true,
For God loves His children and takes care of them, too. . .
And all of His treasures are yours to share
If you love Him completely and show that you care. . .
And if you walk in His footsteps and have faith to believe,
There's nothing you ask for that you will not receive!

Peace I leave with you, my peace I give unto you: not as the world giveth, give I unto you. Let not your heart be troubled, neither let it be afraid.

JOHN 14:27

THE PEACE WE'RE SEEKING

If we but had the eyes to see
God's face in every cloud,
If we but had the ears to hear
His voice above the crowd,
If we could feel His gentle touch
In every springtime breeze
And find a haven in His arms
'Neath sheltering, leafy trees. . .
If we could just lift up our hearts
Like flowers to the sun
And trust His loving promise
And pray, "Thy will be done,"
We'd find the peace we're seeking,
The kind no man can give,
The peace that comes from knowing
He died so we might live!

For God so loved the world, that he gave his only begotten Son, that whosoever believeth in him should not perish, but have everlasting life.

John 3:16

GOD SO LOVED THE WORLD

Our Father up in heaven, long, long years ago,
Looked down in His great mercy upon the earth below
And saw that folks were lonely and lost in deep despair.
And so He said, "I'll send My Son to walk among them there
So they can hear Him speaking and feel His nearness, too,
And see the many miracles that faith alone can do.
For I know it will be easier to believe and understand
If man can see and talk to Him and touch His healing hand."
So whenever we have troubles and we're overcome by cares,
We can take it all to Jesus, for He understands our prayers.

The love of God is shed abroad in our hearts by the Holy Ghost which is given unto us.

ROMANS 5:5

ENFOLDED IN HIS LOVE

The love of God surrounds us
Like the air we breathe around us—
As near as a heartbeat, as close as a prayer,
And whenever we need Him, He'll always be there!

He that dwelleth in the secret place of the most High shall abide under the shadow of the Almighty. I will say of the LORD, He is my refuge and my fortress: my God; in him will I trust.

PSALM 91:1–2

GOD'S LOVE IS LIKE A HAVEN
IN THE STORMS OF LIFE

God's love is like an island in life's ocean vast and wide—
A peaceful, quiet shelter from the restless, rising tide.
God's love is like a fortress, and we seek protection there
When the waves of tribulation seem to drown us in despair.
God's love is like a sanctuary where our souls can find sweet rest
From the struggle and the tension of life's fast and futile quest.
God's love is like a tower rising far above the crowd,
And God's smile is like the sunshine
breaking through the threatening cloud.
God's love is like a beacon burning bright with faith and prayer,
And through all the changing scenes of life
we can find a haven there.
For God's love is fashioned after something enduring
And it is endless and unfailing like His character above.

O give thanks unto the LORD; for he is good;
for his mercy endureth for ever.

1 CHRONICLES 16:34

WHAT MORE CAN YOU ASK?

God's love endures forever—
what a wonderful thing to know
When the tides of life run against you
and your spirit is downcast and low.
God's kindness is ever around you,
always ready to freely impart
Strength to your faltering spirit,
cheer to your lonely heart.
God's presence is ever beside you,
as near as the reach of your hand.
You have but to tell Him your troubles—
there is nothing He won't understand. . .
And knowing God's love is unfailing,
and His mercy unending and great,
You have but to trust in His promise—
"God comes not too soon or too late". . .
So wait with a heart that is patient
for the goodness of God to prevail,
For never do prayers go unanswered,
and His mercy and love never fail.

*I will both lay me down in peace,
and sleep: for thou, LORD,
only makest me dwell in safety.*

PSALM 4:8

NOW I LAY ME DOWN TO SLEEP

I remember so well this prayer I said
Each night as my mother tucked me in bed.
And today this same prayer is still the best way
To sign off with God at the end of the day
And to ask Him your soul to safely keep
As you wearily close your tired eyes in sleep,
Feeling content that the Father above
Will hold you secure in His great arms of love. . .
And having His promise that if ere you wake,
His angels reach down, your sweet soul to take,
In perfect assurance that, awake or asleep,
God is always right there to tenderly keep
All of His children ever safe in His care,
For God's here and He's there and He's everywhere. . .
So into His hands each night as I sleep,
I commend my soul for the dear Lord to keep,
Knowing that if my soul should take flight,
It will soar to the land where there is no night.

Likewise the Spirit also helpeth our infirmities: for we know not what we should pray for as we ought: but the Spirit itself maketh intercession for us with groanings which cannot be uttered.

Romans 8:26

GOD, ARE YOU THERE?

I'm way down here—You're way up there.
Are You sure You can hear my faint, faltering prayer?
For I'm so unsure of just how to pray—
To tell You the truth, God, I don't know what to say.
I just know I'm lonely and vaguely disturbed,
Bewildered and restless, confused and perturbed,
And they tell me that prayer helps to quiet the mind
And to unburden the heart, for in stillness we find
A newborn assurance that Someone does care
And Someone does answer each small, sincere prayer.

Cast thy burden upon the LORD,
and he shall sustain thee: he shall
never suffer the righteous to be moved.

Psalm 55:22

IT'S ME AGAIN, GOD

Remember me, God? I come every day
Just to talk with You, Lord, and to learn how to pray.
You make me feel welcome; You reach out Your hand.
I need never explain, for You understand.
I come to You frightened and burdened with care,
So lonely and lost and so filled with despair,
And suddenly, Lord, I'm no longer afraid—
My burden is lighter and the dark shadows fade.
Oh God, what a comfort to know that You care
And to know when I seek You, You will always be there.

The LORD is good, a strong hold in the day of trouble; and he knoweth them that trust in him.

Nahum 1:7

WELLS OF SALVATION

Oh blessed Father, hear this prayer
And keep us all in Your care.
You are so great. . .we are so small. . .
And when trouble comes as it does to us all
There's so little that we can do
Except to place our trust in You!
So place yourself in His loving care
And He will gladly help you bear
Whatever lies ahead of you.
And God will see you safely through,
For no earthly pain is ever too much
If God bestows His merciful touch.

And thou shalt love the LORD thy
God with all thine heart, and with
all thy soul, and with all thy might.

DEUTERONOMY 6:5

SHOW ME THE WAY TO SERVE
AND LOVE YOU MORE

God, help me in my feeble way
To somehow do something each day
To show You that I love You best
And that my faith will stand each test,
And let me serve You every day
And feel You near me when I pray.
Oh, hear my prayer, dear God above,
And make me worthy of Your love.

I am crucified with Christ: nevertheless I live;
yet not I, but Christ liveth in me: and the
life which I now live in the flesh I live by
the faith of the Son of God, who loved me,
and gave himself for me.

GALATIANS 2:20

A PART OF ME

Dear God, You are a part of me—
You're all I do and all I see;
You're what I say and what I do,
For all my life belongs to You.
You walk with me and talk with me,
For I am Yours eternally,
And when I stumble, slip, and fall
Because I'm weak and lost and small,
You help me up and take my hand
And lead me toward the Promised Land.
I cannot dwell apart from You—
You would not ask or want me to,
For You have room within Your heart
To make each child of Yours a part
Of You and all Your love and care
If we but come to You in prayer.

Trust in him at all times; ye people, pour out your heart before him: God is a refuge for us.

PSALM 62:8

MY DAILY PRAYER

God, be my resting place and my protection
In hours of trouble, defeat, and dejection.
May I never give way to self-pity and sorrow,
May I always be sure of a better tomorrow,
May I stand undaunted come what may,
Secure in the knowledge I have only to pray
And ask my Creator and Father above
To keep me serene in His grace and His love.

Whosoever therefore shall humble himself as this little child, the same is greatest in the kingdom of heaven.

MATTHEW 18:4

A CHILD'S FAITH

"Jesus loves me, this I know,
For the Bible tells me so."
Little children ask no more,
For love is all they're looking for,
And in a small child's shining eyes
The faith of all the ages lies.
And tiny hands and tousled heads
That kneel in prayer by little beds
Are closer to the dear Lord's heart
And of His kingdom more a part
Than we who search and never find
The answers to our questioning minds—
For faith in things we cannot see
Requires a child's simplicity.

The LORD bless thee, and keep thee: the LORD make his face shine upon thee, and be gracious unto thee: the LORD lift up his countenance upon thee, and give thee peace.

NUMBERS 6:24–26

GOD BLESS AND KEEP
YOU IN HIS CARE

There are many things in life
we cannot understand,
But we must trust God's judgment
and be guided by His hand. . .
And all who have God's blessing
can rest safely in His care,
For He promises safe passage
on the wings of faith and prayer.

ABOUT HELEN STEINER RICE

Born in Ohio in 1900, Helen Steiner Rice began writing at an early age. In 1918, Helen took a job at a public utilities company, eventually becoming one of the first female advertising managers and public speakers in the country. At age 29, she married banker Franklin Rice, who committed suicide in 1932, never having recovered mentally and financially from losses incurred during the Great Depression.

Following her husband's death, Helen used her gift of verse to encourage others. Her talents came to the attention of the nation when her greeting card poem "The Priceless Gift of Christmas" was read on the Lawrence Welk Show. Soon a series of poetry books, a source of inspiration to people worldwide, followed. Helen died in 1981, leaving a foundation that offers assistance to the needy and elderly.